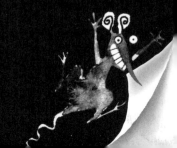

Hazardous
History

First published in Great Britain in 2006
by English Heritage

10 9 8 7 6 5 4 3 2

Design by Peter Wilkinson
Cover illustration by Rowan Barnes-Murphy
Typeset by David Onyett, Publishing & Production Services, Cheltenham
Printed in Thailand by Imago

ENGLISH HERITAGE

Introduction

In the middle of the 17th century the philosopher Thomas Hobbes summed up human existence as a 'continual fear and danger of violent death; and the life of man, solitary, poor, nasty, brutish and short'.

Hobbes could have been describing life for most people 300 years either side of his own day and still have been close to the mark. Life was cheap; life was cruel. And death could come suddenly or carry you away in slow, lingering agony.

Fortunately it is hard for most of us in this country today to imagine the everyday dangers faced by our forebears, quite apart from the noise, smell, dirt and general discomfort that they accepted as their lot in life.

Hazardous History sets out to convey something of the risks people in the past faced simply going about their everyday lives. In many cases it draws on their own words to create a vivid and telling image of what they had to endure and the ways in which they coped with their circumstances.

HaZaRdouS HisToRY

DIGGING UP THE DIRT

The 16th-century Dutch scholar, Erasmus, spent several years in England, during which time he taught at both Oxford and Cambridge universities. Familiar with the homes of the better-off in society, Erasmus was still unimpressed by the state of many of them. Writing in 1518, he noted:

> Floors are strewed with clay, and that covered with rushes which are now and then renewed, but not so as to disturb the foundation, which sometimes remains for twenty years nursing a collection of spittle, vomits, excrements of dogs and human beings, spilt beer and fishes bones and other filth that I need not mention.

THE BLACK DEATH

The Great Plague of 1665 may be the most well known of the epidemics to have hit London, but historically it was significant as the most devastating of a succession of outbreaks of plague that had struck the city since the first recorded epidemic in AD 664. Epidemics occurred in London throughout the Middle Ages, the most catastrophic of which arrived in London in late September 1348 and was rampant throughout the city by November. The Black Death, as it became known from the dark haemorrhaging beneath the skin of victims, is said to have killed half the population of England and an even higher proportion of the people in cities such as London, where crowded filthy streets, cramped living conditions and an almost complete lack of sanitation helped disease spread rapidly. In Southwark alone 200 dead were buried every day at the height of the epidemic and new burial grounds were rapidly dug as the old ones filled to overflowing. In January 1349 the King prorogued Parliament in the face of the crisis. In May the Abbot of the monastery of Westminster and 27 of his monks died and were buried in a mass grave. In the same month all but one of the brothers and sisters of the Hospital of St James also died.

Possibly even more terrifying than the disease itself was the fact that the cause of the disease was unknown. Supernatural forces, the wrath of God, and the coming of the end of the world were all blamed. People tried burning juniper to ward off infection; 'plague tracts' advised the sick to let blood or swallow vinegar. But whatever remedy they tried the sinister black swellings were rapidly followed by high fever, agonising thirst, delirium and death. Five and a half centuries later, the actual cause was identified as infected rats and the fleas they carried.

TOO YOUNG TO DIE

On 4 May 1301 three-year-old Petronilla, daughter of William de Wyntonia, was playing in the street late one day when she was struck by the horse ridden by one Hugh Picard. Try as he might, the rider was unable to hold back his mount, which trampled over the poor little girl and caught her with its right forefoot. 24 hours later the little girl died of her injuries. Hugh Picard fled the scene of the accident, but later thought better of his actions and surrendered himself to the sheriff.

In April 1324 John, the five-year-old son of William de Burgh, stole 'a parcel of wood' from the house of Richard de Latthere and placed it in his cap. The lady of the house, Richard's wife Emma, caught him in the act and in her fury swung a blow that caught the child under the left ear. Hearing her son's cries, the little boy's mother hurried to the scene and carried him away, but there was nothing she could do and her son died later that day.

HaZaRDOUS HISTORY

UNEASY BEDFELLOWS

Between the reigns of Henry VIII and his youngest daughter, Elizabeth I, there was a steady improvement in general household conditions that must have made life a great deal more comfortable. Looking back to his father's day, Parson William Harrison noted in 1577 that a generation earlier most people went to sleep on straw pallets, covered with a sheet, with covers made of rough material; for a pillow a log of wood served as a bolster. Straw bedding was, of course, a fertile breeding ground for plague-carrying fleas. Mattresses and feather pillows were the preserve of the very rich. Servants were lucky if they had a sheet to lie on to provide some protection from pricking straws poking through the canvas covering their straw mattresses.

FOISTERS, NIPPERS AND A SCHOOL FOR SCANDAL

Street crime was so rife in Elizabethan London that one enterprising publican developed a lucrative sideline helping pickpockets refine their craft. Writing in 1581, the Recorder of London described what investigators discovered when they searched his alehouse near Billingsgate.

> There were hung up two devices, the one was a pocket, the other was a purse. The pocket had in it certain counters, and was hung about with hawks' bells, and over the top did hang a little sacring bell [a sanctus bell]; and he that could take out a counter without any noise, was allowed to be a 'public foister' [pickpocket], and he that could take a piece of silver out of the purse without the noise of any of the bells, he was adjudged 'a judicial nipper' [cutpurse].

MOBBED AT THE PILLORY

The pillory was a method of public punishment that remained in use in England for well over 600 years from the 13th to the 19th centuries. Although executions were public spectacles, the pillory gave the general public the chance to mete out punishment for particular types of crime that were thought to be particularly distasteful to the man in the street. So those convicted of offences such as extortion, fraud, perjury, uttering seditious words and sodomy, found themselves sentenced to an hour in the pillory, where they were often at the mercy of a vindictive mob.

In London pillories were set up in busy thoroughfares such as Cheapside and Charing Cross. Here revolving platforms were erected in which convicted criminals could be locked in a wooden structure through which their head and hands protruded. Confined in this way the felon was an inviting target for whatever people chose to throw in his or her direction (though the majority of people sentenced to the pillory were men). Rotten eggs, rotten vegetables, entrails and offal from slaughterhouses, the carcasses of dead animals, mud, excrement and sometimes bricks and stones could rain down on criminals in the pillory. In the worst cases the victim could die under a hail of such missiles, though constables might try in vain to provide a degree of protection. In some cases criminals in the pillory had their noses slit, their faces branded with one or more letters and one or both ears cut off.

Though the use of the pillory was restricted in 1816 to those convicted of perjury, it was not totally abolished as a punishment until 1837.

PRISONERS OF THE INQUISITION

There was little mercy shown between English and Spanish sailors during the reign of Queen Elizabeth I. Prisoners on both sides were liable to receive harsh treatment. In 1568 Miles Phillips was captured in Mexico after disaster struck the ship commanded by John Hawkins, on which he had been serving. Phillips did not return to England until 1583 and after six years of captivity suffered terribly at the hands of the Spanish Inquisition, which began its work in Mexico in 1574. At first Phillips and his fellow English sailors refused to renounce their Protestant faith, but in January 1575 their inquisitors resorted to their most extreme measures to extract confessions and each of the prisoners was tortured on the rack until their resistance was broken.

In most cases they were sentenced to receive a public flogging on horseback of up to 300 lashes, followed by imprisonment and eventual transfer to a Spanish galley where they would spend as many as eight years chained to an oar. Their ordeal began on Good Friday 1575, as Phillips recorded:

> So they being forced to mount up on horseback, naked from the
> middle upwards, were carried to be shewed as a spectacle for all the

people to behold throughout the chief and principal streets of the city; and had the number of stripes appointed to every one of them, most cruelly laid upon their naked bodies with long whips, by sundry men appointed to be executioners thereof...

So this horrible spectacle being shewed round about the city and they returned to the Inquisitor's House, with their backs all gore blood, and swollen with great bumps; they were then taken from their horses and carried again to prison, where they remained until they were sent into Spain to the galleys, there to receive the rest of their martyrdom.

SMOKE CAN DAMAGE YOUR HEALTH

Although chimneys built into walls began to remove smoke from rooms in the second half of the 15th century, progress was slow in many well-to-do homes; the poor had to put up with breathing smoke indoors for centuries to come. Until the arrival of the chimney, halls were heated by centrally positioned braziers. The smoke from these escaped through open windows, when it could. When the windows were closed in cold weather to keep in the warmth and reduce draughts, smoke from the brazier would quickly build up, to the discomfort of everyone forced to inhale it.

FAIR GAME

Annual fairs were a source of rare entertainment for many city dwellers in times gone by. Reflecting the hard lives endured by most of the visitors, many of the attractions had a ghastly fascination. Displays and puppet re-enactments of recent murders could always be relied on to pull in large crowds.

However, visiting a fair laid you open to petty crime on a well-organised scale, as this description shows.

> And before every show were ballad singers bawling their songs. Their principal business at fairs is not, I am told, to sell their ballads so much as to attract a crowd and engage their attention while the scoundrel pickpockets go about their business unwatched (one was caught in the fair while we were there, and for want of a pump, was put head first into a tub of water, and kept there till he was well nigh drowned)...

HOW TO TREAT MALARIA

Anyone suffering from a bout of malaria in the 17th century might have been offered this remedy, which appeared in a medical treatise published in 1682:

> To cure quartans [malaria] and gout, take the hair and nails of the patient, cut them small, and either give them to the birds in a roasted egg or put them in a hole in an oak tree or a plane tree. Stop up the hole with a peg of the same tree.

GALLEY SLAVES

Protestant captives were still being sent to row in foreign galleys as a punishment for their faith a century after Miles Phillips's account. In 1703–4 John Bion witnessed at first hand the horrific conditions suffered by prisoners aboard French galleys. Bion had served as a chaplain aboard a galley plying the waters of what two centuries later would become the playground of the rich along the Riviera, between the ports of Monaco, Antibes and Nice.

HaZaRDOUS HISTORY

It is hard to give an exact description of the pains and labours the slaves undergo at sea, especially during a long campaign. The fatigue of tugging at the oar is extraordinary. They must rise to draw their stroke, and fall back again almost on their backs: insomuch that, in all seasons, through the continual and violent motion of their bodies, the sweat trickles down their harassed limbs.

And for fear they should fail, as they often do through faintness, there is a gang board, which runs through the middle of the ship, on which are constantly posted three Comites, an Officer somewhat like a Boatswain in Her Majesty's ships, who whenever they find or think that an oar does not keep touch with the rest, without ever examining whether it proceeds from weakness or laziness, they unmercifully exercise a tough wand on the man they suspect which being long is often felt by two or three of his innocent neighbours, who being naked when they row, each blow imprints evident marks of the inhumanity of the executioner...

HaZaRDOUS HISTORY

FINGER FOODS

In spite of a sense of growing national prosperity during the reign of Elizabeth I, eating was still a messy business. Forks were unknown and if you couldn't manage the food in front of you with a spoon and knife, you had no choice but to resort to eating with your fingers. The Queen herself was dexterous at picking at a chicken bone by hand.

THE BEAUTIFUL GAME

Games of football in the Middle Ages were chaotic, had few rules and posed a serious risk to anyone caught up in them whether intentionally or by accident. Teams could have any number of players who would clash in a heaving mass as they struggled to propel a ball made from an inflated pig's bladder to markers at each end of a town or village. Any tactic or means could be used to move the ball and football games often resulted in what amounted to pitched battles between opposing sides.

By the 12th century football had become a feature of Shrovetide celebrations. Writing in the late 1170s William FitzStephen recorded a game played by London youths in fields on the outskirts of the city.

> After lunch all the youth of the city go out into the fields to take part in a ball game. The students of each school have their own ball; the workers from each city craft are also carrying their balls. Older citizens, fathers, and wealthy citizens come on horseback to watch their juniors competing, and to relive their own youth vicariously: you can see their inner passions aroused as they watch the action and get caught up in the fun being had by the carefree adolescents.

It was when games of football moved into the narrow streets of towns and cities that they became a menace to onlookers and passers-by as well as the participants. In 1314 a statute issued in the name of Edward II attempted to ban football in London, stating:

> Forasmuch as there is a great noise in the city caused by hustling over large balls, from which many evils may arise, which God forbid, we command and forbid, on behalf of the King, on pain of imprisonment, such game to be used in the city in future.

HaZaRDOUS HISTORY

In 1389 an edict issued in the reign of Richard II again attempted to ban football, though the authorities were less concerned by the noise and 'the many evils' it caused than by the disinclination of the king's subjects to practise archery, which had obvious military value.

The attraction of the game persisted despite royal disapproval. By Tudor times it was still a brutal pastime blamed by the author of the *Anatomie of Abuses* as being the cause of:

> ...fighting, brawling, contention, quarrel picking, murder, homicide. And great effusion of blood, as daily experience teacheth.

TORTURE IN THE TOWER

Fears about Roman Catholic conspiracies against Queen Elizabeth I and her government led to the arrest and execution of many Catholics suspected of plotting against the Queen. In the spring of 1597 a Jesuit named John Gerard was imprisoned in the Tower of London where he was interrogated about his association with Father Henry Garnet, a leading Catholic suspect who was still at large.

Gerard refused to incriminate his fellow Catholics and a warrant was produced authorising the use of torture to make him talk. This is his account of what followed.

We went to the torture room in a kind of solemn procession, the attendants walking ahead with lighted candles.

The chamber was underground and dark, particularly near the entrance. It was a vast place and every device and instrument of human torture was there. They pointed out some of them to me and said that I would try them all. Then they asked me again whether I would confess.

'I cannot,' I said.

I fell on my knees for a moment's prayer. Then they took me to a big upright pillar, one of the wooden posts which held the roof of this huge underground chamber. Driven in to the top of it were iron staples for supporting heavy weights. Then they put my wrists into iron gauntlets and ordered me to climb two or three wicker steps. My arms were then lifted up and an iron bar was passed through the rings of one gauntlet. This done, they fastened the bar with a pin to prevent it slipping, and then, removing the wicker steps one by one from under my feet, they left me hanging by my hands and arms fastened above my head. The tips of my toes, however, still touched the ground, and they had to dig away the earth from under them. They had hung me from the highest staple in the pillar and could not raise me any higher, without driving in another staple.

Hanging like this I began to pray. The gentlemen standing around asked me whether I was willing to confess now.

'I cannot and I will not,' I answered.

But I could hardly utter the words, such a gripping pain came over me. It was worst in my chest and belly, my hands and arms. All the blood in my body seemed to rush up into my arms and hands and I thought that blood was oozing out from the ends of my fingers and pores of my skin.

Gerard was left hanging like this for upwards of five hours. Whenever he fainted (and he passed out eight or nine times during the afternoon) his weight was supported by his tormentors until he came round, when they let him hang from his wrists once more. He was taken down and returned to his cell but the following morning, when he again refused to disclose the whereabouts of Father Garnet, John Gerard was handed over to a man described as the Master of Torture, who was ordered to torture the prisoner twice a day until he confessed.

> The man took charge of me. Wade [Gerard's principal interrogator] left. In the same way as before we went to the torture chamber.
>
> The gauntlets were placed on the same part of my arms as last time. They would not fit anywhere else, because the flesh on either side had swollen into small mounds, leaving a furrow between; and the gauntlets could only be fastened in the furrow. I felt a very sharp pain when they were put on.
>
> But God helped me and I gladly offered Him my hands and my heart. I was hung up in the same way as before, but now I felt a much severer pain in my hands but less in my chest and belly. Possibly this was because I had eaten nothing that morning...
>
> This time it was longer before I fainted, but when I did they found it so difficult to bring me round that they thought that I was dead, or certainly dying, and summoned the Lieutenant.

After being taken down to regain consciousness, Gerard again refused to talk and was hung up for a third time. In spite of his weakness and agony he refused to denounce his associates. His stoicism paid off and he was subjected to no further torture; six months later he was fit enough to escape, using a rope suspended over the Tower ditch.

SHIPWRECKED ON SCILLY

In October 1707 five ships carrying over 2,000 troops and sailors, under the command of Admiral Sir Clowdisley Shovell, were sailing into the Western Approaches of the English Channel. Spirits were high: Sir Clowdisley's men had been engaged in successful operations against French forces in the Mediterranean and they were on their way home. Then the weather closed in. Fog blanketed the ships for twelve days and most on board had no idea where they were. This was not uncommon. In fact positions at sea had been largely a matter of guesswork ever since sailors had ventured out of sight of land for any length of time. The problem was in calculating longitude: the distance east or west of a known position, or meridian. So Sir Clowdisley's navigation officers put their heads together and concluded that they were safely west of the island of Ouessant, lying off the Brittany peninsula. If they were right, open sea lay ahead of them and the fleet continued sailing northwards.

Sadly, their calculations were well wide of the mark. Though west of Ouessant, the fleet was also a good hundred miles north of the island and therefore close to the northern edge of the Western Approaches. It was not rocky outcrops around Ouessant that should have been their concern, but the reef-strewn waters of the Isles of Scilly, 20 miles from Land's End, off the south-west tip of Cornwall. On the night of 22 October, Sir Clowdisley's ships smashed straight into Scilly's Western Rocks. The admiral's flagship, the *Association* hit the rocks first and sank in minutes. The *Eagle* and the *Romney* were next to go down, unable to react in time to what had happened. That terrible night four of Sir Clowdisley's five ships were sunk, taking to the bottom with them over 1,500 men.

Only two survivors made it ashore. Sir Clowdisley was one of them, but he suffered a fate suffered by many shipwrecked mariners. Legend has it that, half-drowned and exhausted, Sir Clowdisley was murdered on the shoreline by a local woman who took a fancy to the large emerald ring he was wearing.

The tragedy of Sir Clowdisley's lost fleet led to a scientific drive to find an accurate means of measuring longitude to end such disasters at sea. But it took over 60 years for that to be achieved and thousands more seamen lost their lives until they were able to sail the oceans confident of where they were.

BLOODY SLIM

From the 18th to the early 20th centuries it was fashionable for women to have absurdly thin waistlines, some as narrow as 18 inches. For most women, even those who were naturally slim, this was impossible to achieve without the use of a corset worn beneath elegant outer garments. So fashionable women had to go through the discomfort of being laced into a tight-fitting corset that squeezed and compressed their torsos into the desired shape. Corsets were made of strong materials and many were stiffened with whalebone and steel. Once a woman was laced into her corset, bending over became almost impossible. Even so women were still expected to wear corsets when they were taking exercise such as riding or playing tennis. Elizabeth Ryan, who was a very successful tennis doubles player, described a typical dressing room in a tennis club before the First World War. Most clubs provided a rail near the fireplace where women could dry the corsets they had worn while playing on court. It was never a pretty sight, Elizabeth Ryan recalled, because most of the corsets were bloodstained.

The damage caused by wearing tight corsets over a long period is likely to have extended well below the skin. Modern writers claim that corsets caused severe damage to women's spinal cords and internal organs.

GOOD BOOK – BAD BOOK

Although there was a strong demand for books of religious instruction in the 15th century, few people had access to the most important Christian book of all – the Bible. In fact possessing a Bible without an appropriate licence to have one could land the owner in serious trouble with the Church authorities, who often saw owning an unlicensed Bible as a sign of heresy, punishable in the most extreme cases by burning at the stake.

RING-A-RING O'ROSES

London was little better prepared to face the Great Plague of 1665 than it had been when the city had been struck by the Black Death over three centuries earlier. Again infected rats and their fleas spread the disease throughout the city that now had a population many times greater than it had in the middle of the 14th century. A spell of bitterly cold weather from November 1664 until March 1665, during which the Thames froze, had kept the plague at bay. When the weather warmed in the spring of 1665, the number of its victims rose inexorably week by week. As the summer wore on grave-diggers working in shifts were unable to keep up with the volume of dead to be buried. Bodies were stacked in the streets for two or three days and even when they were interred, in some plague pits the upper layer of corpses was covered by only a few inches of soil, so that the air was filled with the stench of decomposing flesh. Added to this was the smell of the putrefying animal carcasses that littered the streets, swelling up and bursting in the summer sun.

When the plague was confirmed in a household, every member was locked inside the house for 40 days once the infected had either recovered or died. Armed guards were stationed outside day and night, to make sure no one inside emerged; though conditions inside these barred dwellings became so appalling that sympathetic neighbours sometimes drove away the guards and tore down the notices warning about the plague.

Many fled London altogether, though they became unwelcome arrivals in other places to which they fled. Thousands of Londoners wandered aimlessly from one place to another, driven away under barrages of stones and manure. Others took to living aboard boats moored in the Thames, where the casualty rate was lower.

By the middle of September over 8,000 people a week were dying in London, though the figures were estimated by some to be as high as 14,000. The Great Plague had reached its peak and as autumn turned to winter the numbers dying in the city started to decline. By the beginning of February 1666, King Charles II felt it was safe to return to his capital which in a matter of months would be consumed in the Great Fire.

Approaching 100,000 people had died of the plague in London in 1665. The symptoms of the disease were summed up in the nursery rhyme:

HaZaRDOUS HISTORY

Ring-a-ring o'roses
A pocket full of posies
A-tishoo! A-tishoo!
We all fall down.

The 'roses' referred to were the rosy rash that gave the first sign of infection. This was followed by the appearance of the 'ring' of swellings that confirmed the plague. Some people carried 'posies' of herbs and spices to sweeten the air. And sneezing ('A-tishoo! A-tishoo!') was a symptom often associated with those close to death.

THE SCOURGE OF SCURVY

Until the importance of vitamin C was recognised, sailors on extended voyages far from land and deprived of supplies of fresh fruit and vegetables were prey to the terrible disease of scurvy.

In the early 1740s Richard Walker sailed round the world and recorded the impact of scurvy on the crew of the ship in which he was travelling. 43 of the crew died of scurvy in April 1741 and almost twice as many in May. It was not until mid-June that they made land, by which time scurvy had claimed more than 200 and, as Walker noted, the ship's company 'could not at last master more than six fore-mast men in a watch capable of duty'.

> These common appearances [of scurvy, Walker continued] are large discoloured spots dispersed over the whole surface of the body, swelled legs, putrid gums, and above all, an extraordinary lassitude of the whole body, especially after any exercise, however inconsiderable; and this lassitude at last degenerates into a proneness of swoon on the least exertion of strength, or even on the least motion...
>
> At other times the whole body, but more especially the legs, were subject to ulcers of the worst kind, attended with rotten bones, and such a luxuriancy of fungous flesh, as yielded to no remedy. But a most extraordinary circumstance, and what would be scarcely credible upon any single evidence, is, that the scars of wounds which had been for many years healed, were forced open again by this virulent distemper.

MARRY FOR LOVE, LOVE WHERE THERE'S MONEY

Courtly love in the Middle Ages existed for the most part in verse and song. The reality of love and courtship was rather more hard-nosed, with marriage invariably being a means to financial and social gain. It was quite common among the nobility for marriages to be arranged between 'bride' and 'groom' when they were still small children. Once pledged to each other they were united for life, bargaining chips for their parents to exploit as they wished.

If any child resisted marrying under these conditions, parents resorted to corporal punishment to persuade them to see the error of their ways. The records of the Paston family, who lived in the Norfolk village of Paston in the 15th century, showed that one daughter, Elizabeth, refused (not unnaturally for a young girl) to marry an unprepossessing widower aged 50. It took her mother three months to make her change her mind, during which time the girl was 'beaten once in the week or twice, sometimes twice in one day and her head broken in two or three places'.

Medieval girls who could not be married off often found themselves placed in nunneries. Families wanting to rid themselves of unmarried offspring and relatives were expected to make suitable donations to nunneries, in exchange for a permanent home for the ladies in question.

HOLDING YOUR TONGUE

Women were not encouraged to speak their minds in 17th- and 18th-century England. Those who had the temerity to say what they thought or, worse still, criticise their husbands, risked more than a telling off. As scolds, a special punishment designed to humiliate as well as cause pain had been devised to correct their ways. This was a metal cage-like device called a branks, which could be locked over a woman's head to teach her a lesson.

The branks was made of iron and included a muzzle that was clamped down over the woman's tongue to prevent her talking. This tongue plate was often fitted with sharp spikes which cut into the soft tissue of the tongue with the slightest movement. Once fitted with the branks, the scold, or shrew as she was often known, would be paraded publicly. Pulled along like a pack animal by a halter attached to the branks, any tug on the halter, even a sudden movement of the head, could cause sharp, stinging pain to her tongue – a caution to more careful about how she used it in the future.

BEWARE! ARCHERS!

It was a good idea to keep clear of places where archery practice took place in medieval England. This was a serious business and archers were a cornerstone of national defence. In fact the importance of having a corps of skilled archers in medieval England was recognised by an Act of 1369 that encouraged the citizens of London to keep up their archery practice: 'that everyone of the said City of London strong in body at leisure times and on holidays, use in their recreation bows and arrows'.

The power of a longbow can be devastating, as English victories at battles such as Crécy in 1346 and Agincourt in 1415 conclusively proved. War arrows fitted with vicious tips were capable of penetrating thick wooden doors and an archer who accidentally killed anyone in the course of practising invariably escaped without punishment.

CAPTAIN COOK AND THE 'BLOODY FLUX'

Captain Cook's first voyage of discovery in 1768–71 aboard the *Endeavour* was remarkable not only because of its scientific and geographical achievements, but because of the remarkable well-being of the crew for much of their arduous voyage. On their arrival at Batavia, Sir Joseph Banks, the principal naturalist on the voyage, noted how ill seamen aboard other ships looked compared with the *Endeavour*'s crew: 'our people however who truly might be called rosy and plump, for we had not a sick man among us, jeered and flaunted much at their brother seamen's white faces'.

Their amusement was short-lived, however. Malaria, endemic in Batavia, soon struck down most of the crew, including the captain. This weakened their health and when they were at sea again bound for the Cape of Good Hope, dysentery (or 'the bloody flux' as it was termed by seafarers) spread through the ship. 23 men died on the 11-week voyage to South Africa. Two more died on the return voyage to England and when Captain Cook submitted his report to the Admiralty there were 19 men described as 'sick' out of a total complement of 82. The condition of the ship at the end of the voyage was summed up by its captain in the single word 'foul'.

A LOT OF WHAT YOU FANCY

Although Londoners had access to a wider range of food than people in other parts of the country, their diet was not necessarily any healthier. Fruit and vegetables featured little at mealtimes and dairy produce was less widely consumed than in rural areas. Bread, pastries, fish, poultry and sweetmeats filled the bellies of Londoners who could afford to eat well. This may account for one description of London women as 'sweetly pretty but for their black teeth'.

CRIME IN KENSINGTON

Even though London was expanding in the middle of the 18th century the city had still miles to spread in every direction to achieve its present-day size. Kensington, for instance, was praised in 1705 by the author of

Antiquities of Middlesex for its degree of sophistication. In his judgement, Kensington 'is inhabited by gentry and persons of note; there is also an abundance of shopkeepers and...artificers...which makes it appear rather like a part of London than a country village.' In 1749 the affluent, but still detached status that Kensington enjoyed made it the haunt of criminals, as *The London Evening Post* reported in November 1749:

> On Wednesday night last, as the Hon. Mr. Horace Walpole, Brother to the Right Hon. the Earl of Orford, was returning from Holland-House, between Nine and Ten, he was stopt in Hyde-Park by Two Men on Horseback, mask'd, one of which held a Blunderbuss to the Coachman, while the other came up to the Chariot, and, thrusting a Pistol into it, demanded Mr. Walpole's Money and Watch; he gave the Fellow his Purse, and as he was giving him the Watch, the Pistol, which was held close to his Cheek, went off; but, tho' it was so near that the Force struck Mr. Walpole backwards, the ball luckily miss'd him, and went thro' the Corner of the Chariot just above his Head, only scorching his Face, and leaving several marks of Powder. The Coachman started,

and said, What is that? The Man with the Blunderbuss swore he would shoot him, if he spoke, bid him give him his Watch, and then riding up to the Chariot, they took Mr. Walpole's Sword, and some Silver from the Footman, and rode off to Kensington Gate. Besides the two Highwaymen who attacked the Chariot of Horace Walpole, Esq: there were three more at a Distance, who waited the Event, very strongly arm'd.

KEEP IT IN THE FAMILY – DEATH FROM CHOLERA

In the cramped, unhygienic surroundings in which slum-dwellers lived in the first half of the 19th century, outbreaks of cholera could be devastating. In 1832 the physician Sir James Kay-Shuttleworth recorded what happened to a poor Irish family living beside the 'black, polluted stream' of the river Medlock in Manchester.

He had been called to see the father of the family whose health was declining so rapidly that he died only a matter of hours after taking to his bed. His widow and three children were immediately taken to a cholera hospital, where Kay-Shuttleworth visited them later that same day.

The Knott Hill Hospital was a cotton factory stripped of its machinery, and furnished with iron bedsteads and bedding on every floor. On my arrival here I found the widow and her three children with a nurse grouped round a fire at one end of a gloomy ward. I ascertained that all necessary arrangements had been made for their comfort. They had an evening meal; the children were put to bed near the fire, except the infant which I left lying upon its mother's lap. None of them showed any sign of disease, and I left the ward to take some refreshment. On my return, or at a later visit before midnight, the infant had been sick in its mother's lap, had made a faint cry and had died. The mother was naturally full of terror and distress, for the child had had no medicine, had been fed only from its mother's breast, and, consequently, she could have no doubt that it perished from the same cause as its father. I sat with her and the nurse by the fire very late into the night. While I was there the children did not wake, nor seem in any way disturbed, and at length I thought I myself might seek some repose. When I returned about six o'clock in the morning, another child had severe cramps with some sickness, and while I stood by the bedside, it died. Then, later, the third and eldest child had all the characteristic symptoms of cholera and perished in one or two hours. In the course of the day the mother likewise suffered from a severe and rapid succession of the characteristic symptoms and died, so that within twenty-four hours the whole family was extinct, and it was known that many other cases of cholera had occurred in Manchester or its vicinity.

SENTENCED TO A FLOGGING

Discipline in the Royal Navy of the 18th and early 19th centuries was maintained by a stern regime of corporal punishment. Sailors caught shirking their work could expect to be lashed across the back by a bosun's mate wielding a rattan cane or a length of rope. More serious offences could result in being flogged in front of the whole ship's company.

Men were routinely sentenced to 72 lashes by their captains and the most serious offenders, found guilty of crimes such as desertion, could expect as many as 300. These were carried out by the bosun's mate with a whip known as a cat o'nine tails. A new cat was made for each flogging and comprised a rope handle two feet long, to which were attached nine two-feet-long tails made from quarter-inch thick line. When finished a cat o'nine tails wielded by a man of normal strength could break a piece of inch-square pine (as thick as an average stair banister) with a single blow. A flogging proceeded in sets of 12 lashes, each set being laid on after a change of bosun's mate. It did not take many sets for the victim's back to be whipped to a bruised and bloody pulp that resembled scorched and blackened meat.

Theft aboard ship was punished particularly severely and in the most serious cases each line of the cat was knotted, with three knots spaced three inches apart, to inflict even more painful and damaging wounds.

The majority of floggings were carried out on the offender's own ship. On occasions, however, when a wider example needed to be set, flogging round the fleet was ordered. The number of lashes was divided between the number of ships in port and the sailor sentenced to be flogged was rowed from ship to ship, so that the crew of each vessel could witness his ordeal.

HaZaRDOUS HISTORY

YOU ARE WHAT YOU EAT

Even apparently fresh food had to be treated with caution in the centuries before acceptable standards of hygiene could be enforced. Some shopkeepers were not above adulterating their produce: chalk and sand were added to flour and milk was commonly watered down. Fruit and vegetables could be particularly hazardous. Barges that delivered consignments of 'fresh produce' to London, for example, used to carry sewage on their return trips – and this sewage was spread over the fields where the vegetables were grown to fertilise them.

Buying meat required a strong stomach in the days when the animals were killed on the premises in a stinking slaughterhouse where blood and unused portions of carcasses were collected in a filthy cesspool.

CARTED OFF TO EXECUTION

Public executions often drew large crowds who enjoyed the ghoulish sight of the condemned arriving at the scaffold and often suffering a prolonged, agonising death. The Swiss traveller, César de Saussure, wrote of his experience of viewing an execution at Tyburn in the late 1720s.

> Criminals are not executed immediately after their trial, as they are abroad, but are given several days to prepare for death. During that time they may ask for anything that they require either for the soul or for the body. The chaplain of the prison (for there is one) does not leave them, and offers every consolation in his power. The day before the execution those who desire it may receive the sacrament, provided the chaplain thinks that they have sincerely repented and are worthy of it. On the day of execution the condemned prisoners, wearing a sort of white linen shirt over their clothes and a cap on their heads, are tied two together and placed on carts with their backs to the horses' tails. These carts are guarded and surrounded by constables and other police officers on horseback, each armed with a sort of pike. In this way part of the town is crossed and Tyburn, which is a good half-mile from the last suburb, is reached, and here stands the gibbet. One often sees criminals going to their deaths perfectly unconcerned, others so impenitent that they fill

themselves full of liquor and mock at those who are repentant. When all the prisoners arrive at their destination they are made to mount on a very wide cart made expressly for the purpose, a cord is passed round their necks and the end fastened to the gibbet, which is not very high. The chaplain who accompanies the condemned men is also on the cart; he makes them pray and sing a few verses of the Psalms. The relatives are permitted to mount the cart and take farewell. When the time is up – that is to say about a quarter of an hour – the chaplain and relations get off the cart, the executioner covers the eyes and faces of the prisoners with their caps, lashes the horses that draw the cart, which slips from under the condemned men's feet, and in this way they remain all hanging together.

You often see friends and relations tugging at the hanging men's feet so that they should die quicker and not suffer. The bodies and clothes of the dead belong to the executioner; relatives must, if they wish for them, buy them from him, and unclaimed bodies are sold to surgeons to be dissected. You see most amusing scenes between the people who do not like the bodies to be cut up and the messengers the surgeons have sent for the bodies; blows are given and returned before they can be got away, and sometimes the populace often come to blows as to who will carry the bought corpses to the parents who are waiting.

TEETH TO TAKE YOUR BREATH AWAY

For most people in the 17th and 18th centuries teeth were a problem. If you didn't clean them, they decayed, caused terrible bad breath and either rotted away or had to be pulled out. Cleaning them wasn't much more successful in the long run. Many of the tooth powders in use at that time contained abrasive material such as ground pumice stone and cuttlefish. These would certainly have cleaned plaque from teeth, but they also wore away tooth enamel, exposing teeth to infection and decay.

When a tooth became infected some 'operators for the teeth' attempted to kill the nerve in the diseased tooth by cauterising it with a red-hot spike, and then applying strong acid to make it fall apart by itself. If this wasn't successful the only relief from terrible toothache was extracting the diseased tooth with a pair of large pliers and without any anaesthetic.

HaZaRDous HISTORY

It wasn't uncommon for people to lose so many teeth that their faces became hollow-cheeked, which made them look old before their time. To overcome this, cork pads called 'plumpers' were worn inside the mouth to restore cheeks to their normal shape. That took care of appearance, but chewing food required false teeth. These could come from a variety of sources. Teeth implants from human donors could be inserted into sockets vacated by extracted teeth. Battlefield casualties provided a supply of young and generally healthy teeth. Plagues, such as the Great Plague that struck London in 1665, also supplied a glut of human teeth – though they brought with them the risk of deadly infection. But fixing these implants was hit and miss and they tended to fall out, or become loose, allowing gum disease to flare up.

False teeth made from elephant ivory, ox bone or hippo tusk were popular, though ivory tended to turn yellow after a time. George Washington, first president of the United States of America and one of the most famous wearers of dentures in the 18th century, owned a set made from animal teeth and ivory. In 1781 he wrote a letter to his supplier asking for a set of pliers to tighten the wires that held the dentures in place, and also a scraper to clean the teeth. However, his letter was intercepted by the British, against whom Washington was conducting the American War of Independence, and his request for dental supplies probably went unanswered.

Whatever measures people employed to cope with their teeth, few could deal with the problem of bad breath caused by infected teeth or gums. In the 18th century fans became popular among women of fashion and one theory is that they were used to waft away unpleasant oral odours when people were talking in close proximity.

CARELESS WORDS COST

Attacks on travellers by highwaymen were often prompted by tip-offs from unscrupulous servants working in inns where travellers stayed during their arduous journeys. For centuries anyone travelling with money or other valuables had to be wary of who carried their luggage and of any questions they were asked about their route and destination. Inn servants working in league with highwaymen became practised in handling luggage and judging by its weight whether or not it contained coinage. Although a robbery might not take place at an inn itself, so preserving its good reputation, many hold-ups on the open road resulted from information secretly passed to highwaymen from inns along the way.

TO BATHE, OR NOT TO BATHE

There was little encouragement for people to wash in the early Middle Ages, judging by the soap available to anyone with a mind to freshen themselves up. Alkaline collected from wood ash was boiled with scraps of animal fat. To this mixture human urine was added as a water softener: the urine had to be stored for some time to become suitably potent to serve its purpose. At one time urine was the most used detergent. As well as being an ingredient in soap, urine was collected and used for washing garments, particularly those that needed to be kept white. The major component of urine is ammonia, which is, of course, still used in many cleaning products today.

By many accounts Queen Elizabeth I had a sensitive nose that must have been affronted by the pervading odours of her day. Perfumes and rosewater helped the wealthy mask their own natural aromas and the queen herself set the remarkable example of bathing once a month, 'whether she require it or no' according to one amazed courtier.

STUDENT UNREST

University studies in the Middle Ages were not the tranquil pursuit that quiet cloisters and college gardens might suggest today. Pitched battles between students and townspeople took place during the 14th century in which both sides fought with swords, daggers and even bows and arrows. After a massacre of students and minor clergy at Oxford in 1355, the university closed down until the King stepped in to support it. 26 years later 'town and gown' riots in Cambridge saw the destruction of the university's charters and records.

CHOLERA IN THE CAPITAL

Disease was an ever-present menace in Victorian streets, especially in overcrowded areas of the nation's great cities. In the summer and autumn of 1849 a devastating outbreak of cholera struck the population of central London; out of 30,000 cases, 14,000 died. In October of that year the author Charles Kingsley described the dreadful plight of people he saw in a letter to his wife:

> I was yesterday over the cholera districts of Bermondsey; and, Oh God! What I saw! People having no water to drink – hundreds of them – except the water of the common sewer which stagnates full of dead fish, cats and dogs, under their windows.

In his observation, Kingsley reflected a widely-held belief that cholera arose from an aerial poison produced by the putrefaction of bodies or rotting vegetation. It was only later proved beyond doubt that cholera was a waterborne disease that spread rapidly in polluted water supplies.

TAKING POT LUCK

Cooking and eating for the poorest people in society remained virtually unchanged for hundreds of years. For breakfast a thin gruel made of oats started their day, while other meals were catered for by a stew or pottage, made from whatever could be thrown into the cooking pot, and a little homemade bread. The same cooking pot served other functions: it was used to give clothes an occasional wash and also provided water for the family's annual bath.

KEEL-HAULING

Among the most brutal punishments once meted out in the Royal Navy was the savage and frequently fatal act of keel-hauling. Seamen unfortunate, or guilty, enough to be sentenced to a keel-hauling were bound securely and then thrown over the side of a ship, so that they could be literally hauled underneath the hull from one side to the other.

In addition to the strong chance of drowning, keel-hauling subjected its victims to terrible lacerations from the barnacle-encrusted timbers below the waterline. The sight of a victim emerging from a keel-hauling bleeding, unconscious if he was lucky, though more than likely dead, helped preserve the harsh discipline aboard ship in the 18th and 19th centuries.

STUDENTS OF CRIME

Medieval students were forbidden to take athletic exercise by their university authorities, though visits to taverns and brothels went more or less unchecked. In the worst cases this lack of discipline led to gangs of so-called students roaming the countryside behaving like thieves and bandits.

After the ill-discipline of previous centuries, universities cracked down hard on their students in the 15th and 16th centuries and in the most serious cases students could be given a flogging for breaking university rules.

PRISON, PUNISHMENT AND PRIVATION

Receiving a prison sentence in even the late Georgian period was a degrading and dangerous punishment for what would often be considered petty crimes today. One example of the conditions in which most prisoners lived comes from the political activist Francis Place, who described his experience of visiting Newgate Prison in the mid-1790s.

> In 1794 I was several times in Newgate on visits to persons confined for libel &c – one Sunday in particular I was there when several respectable women were also there – relatives of those I went to see. When the time for leaving the prison arrived we came in a body of nine or ten persons into a large yard which we had to cross – into this yard a number of felons were admitted and they were in such a condition that we were obliged to request the jailer to compel them to tie up their rags so as to conceal their bodies which were most indecently exposed and was I have no doubt intentional to alarm the women and extort money from the men. When they had made themselves somewhat decent we came into the yard, and were pressed upon and almost hussled by the felons whose arms and

voices demanding money made a frightful noise and alarmed the women. I who understood these matters collected all the halfpence I could and by throwing a few at a time over the heads of the felons set them scrambling swearing all but fighting whilst the women and the rest made their way as quickly as possible across the yard.

WALLPAPER TO DIE FOR

In the 19th century doctors began to notice that people were suffering from arsenic poisoning for reasons that were hard, sometimes impossible, to explain. Some victims died; others recovered after being seriously ill. The natural assumption was that these people had been poisoned deliberately, although in many cases this was very difficult to prove. It wasn't until 1893, after nearly a century of mysterious arsenic deaths and illnesses, that an explanation was found. The poisoner had been at work throughout Europe and as far away as the isolated Atlantic island of St Helena. In fact it was on St Helena that the most famous victim, Napoleon Bonaparte, had died. Conspiracy theories blamed either the British establishment or the French royal family for his death in 1821. However,

72 years later the real villain was identified by an Italian biochemist named Bartolomeo Gosio. He showed conclusively that the arsenic in Napoleon's body, and that of every other person who had been mysteriously poisoned, had not been administered by human hands. According to Gosio, the arsenic had come from wallpaper – more precisely, it had come from a bright green pigment used to colour wallpaper.

Gosio discovered that if the wallpaper contained Scheele's Green, as the pigment was known, and became damp and then mouldy, the mould could undergo a chemical reaction that produced a poisonous vapour formed from copper arsenite. The wallpaper in Napoleon's house on St Helena contained Scheele's Green and when the records were examined it was clear that other people in the house had also suffered from 'bad air'. Their symptoms included stomach pains, diarrhoea, swollen limbs and shivering; Napoleon's butler had even died and the emperor had suffered several of the symptoms of arsenic poisoning. Although the cause of his death was probably stomach cancer, the arsenic vapour from mouldy wallpaper inevitably hastened his end, as it did that of many others. People were still dying of what became known as Gosio's Disease well into the

20th century. This was largely as a result of living in damp, poorly ventilated rooms where the wallpaper mould could flourish and discharge its lethal vapour.

NOT FAR FROM THE MADDING CROWD

Any notion that life in the towns and cities of the past was more tranquil than it is today is dispelled by the catalogue of noises commonly found in the narrow streets. London's Thames Street, the major thoroughfare into the city from the wharves beside the river, narrowed in places to eleven feet from side to side, and many other streets similarly restricted the easy movement of goods traffic. This meant that arguments regularly erupted between the drivers of heavily-laden carts and drays as to who had the right of way. Often their draught animals would join in the argument, adding to the noise on the cobbles or rough-paved roadway made by their hooves and the iron-shod wheels of the vehicles they pulled, crashing and squeaking on their laborious way. Other animals, principally livestock on their way to slaughter, had to be driven through narrow streets, complaining no doubt and being driven on by the cries of their handlers. The noise from regular herds of cattle and pigs, flocks of sheep, and upwards of 1,000 turkeys crammed into the streets along with pedestrians, horses, carriages and other vehicles can only be imagined. And all of this was quite apart from the sound of human activities that came from windows and doorways, filling working hours with the din of every kind of industry and entertainment.

BLOOD, BROADSIDES AND BRAVERY

Naval battles in the great age of sail were gory and terrifying – even for the victors. On 1 August 1798 Nelson achieved one of his greatest victories at the Battle of the Nile, a conflict recorded by John Nichol, a member of a gun crew aboard the British ship *Goliath*.

> When we ceased firing, I went on deck to view the state of the fleets, and an awful sight it was. The whole bay was covered with dead bodies, mangled, wounded, and scorched, not a bit of clothes on them except their trousers...
>
> The only incidents I heard of are two. One lad was stationed by

a salt-box, on which he sat to give out cartridges, and keep the lid close – it is a trying berth – when asked for a cartridge, he gave none, yet he sat upright; his eyes were open. One of the men gave him a push; he fell all his length on the deck. There was not a blemish on his body. Yet he was quite dead, and was thrown overboard. The other, a lad who had the match in his hand to fire his gun. In the act of applying it, a shot took off his arm; it hung by a small piece of skin. The match fell to the deck. He looked to his arm, and seeing what had happened, seized the match in his left hand, and fired off the gun before he went to the cockpit to have it dressed. They were in our mess, or I might never have heard of it. Two of them were killed, and I knew not of it until the day after. Thus terminated the glorious first of August, the busiest night of my life.

ON THE SPIKE

Life for the down-and-outs in London at the beginning of the 20th century was as grim then as it is for the city's homeless and destitute today. The writer Jack London had personal experience of life as a tramp in London at the end of the 19th century, which he recounted in *People of the Abyss*. His account of a 'spike', where nightly shelter of sort could be found, is a vivid reminder of the bleak, insanitary conditions in which the poorest in society lived and died surrounded by dirt and disease.

> The light was very dim down in the cellar, and before I knew it some other man had thrust a pannikin into my other hand. Then I stumbled on to a still darker room, where were benches and tables and men. The place smelled vilely, and the sombre gloom, and the mumble of voices from out of the obscurity, made it seem more like some anteroom to the infernal regions.
>
> Most of the men were suffering from tired feet, and they prefaced the meal by removing their shoes and unbinding the filthy rags with which their feet were wrapped. This added to the general noisomeness, while it took away from my appetite...
>
> By seven o'clock we were called away to bathe and go to bed. We stripped our clothes, wrapping them up in our coats and buckling our belts about them, and deposited them in a heaped rack and on the floor—a beautiful scheme for the spread of vermin. Then, two

by two, we entered the bathroom. There were two ordinary tubs, and this I know: the two men preceding had washed in that water, we washed in the same water, and it was not changed for the two men that followed us. This I know; but I am also certain that the twenty-two of us washed in the same water.

I did no more than make a show of splashing some of this dubious liquid at myself, while I hastily brushed it off with a towel wet from the bodies of other men. My equanimity was not restored by seeing the back of one poor wretch a mass of blood from attacks of vermin and retaliatory scratching.

LIVING UNDER A FEUDAL YOKE

After the Norman invasion the feudal law of the manor imposed throughout England made life harder than ever for the great majority of the population, who were serfs to the lord of the manor. Serfs were effectively bonded labour and were legally tied to the land they farmed. And they had little legal right to their children either; no serf could give his or her children in marriage without first obtaining their lord's permission.

STAND AND DELIVER

In 1726, the last year of the reign of George I, Monsieur César de Saussure, a Swiss visitor to Great Britain, wrote to his family describing the hazards that awaited travellers along roads where highwaymen were at large.

They were usually well mounted, he explained, and daring; a single highwayman often holding up a coach with six or seven passengers. With a pistol in one hand and his hat in the other, the highwayman would make the request that has entered folklore as 'Your money or your life'. Few people gave much thought to this choice and those who made some move to disarm their assailant risked being killed or wounded (a fate that frequently ended in death anyway in the 18th century). Most people held up in this way handed over their purses and the highwayman galloped away.

M de Saussure was clearly impressed by the courtesy some highwaymen showed to the people they robbed: 'I have been told that some highwaymen are quite polite and generous, begging to be excused for being forced to rob, and leaving passengers the wherewithal to continue their journey.'

However, he did end his remarks with the stark acknowledgement, 'All highwaymen that are caught are hanged without mercy.'

DEATHLY PALE

For 200 years from the 16th century to the end of the 18th, being beautiful meant being pale, very pale. Only peasants who worked outside had the kind of suntanned complexions fashionable today. Wealthy women had been using cosmetics for thousands of years and one that made a big comeback in the 16th century was white lead, which had been popular in the Roman period before falling out of favour. White lead, or ceruse as it was widely known, was made from lead carbonate or oxide, sometimes with the addition of lemon juice and vinegar. It was spread over the skin of the face, neck and bosom to whiten the complexion. And because it clung well to the skin, it could be applied as a very thin mask, unlike other, cheaper cosmetics that needed to be painted on as a thick layer.

Although white lead was successful in making the wearer look pale, it was also extremely poisonous. Women who wore it regularly suffered from terrible skin problems and as the poison penetrated their bodies other serious health problems arose. Wearers of white lead make-up were not the only ones to suffer. White lead could poison you if it got into your mouth and men who spent too long kissing women wearing white lead could be poisoned and die just as easily as the objects of their desire.

Other poisonous substances were widely used in cosmetics in the past. Arsenic was popular, because it normally occurs as a white mineral that could be used to whiten the skin. The same was true of bismuth, though using this as a cosmetic had an added risk. As well as being poisonous, bismuth could also undergo a chemical reaction if it was exposed to sulphur in the atmosphere. When this happened the white bismuth powder could turn black. Since coal produces sulphur when it is burned, anyone wearing bismuth make-up risked their beautiful pale complexion turning black if they spent too long in a room with a coal fire.

LOST AT SEA

One of the gruesome facts about life in the Royal Navy in the 18th and 19th centuries is that accidents and disease killed more men than shipwrecks or enemy action – and this is in spite of the many historic naval battles fought in this period.

In the most momentous sea battle of all, Trafalgar, fought in 1805, there were, according the naval historian William James, 449 men killed and 1,241 wounded. At the Battle of the Nile (1798), the casualty figures were only half those at Trafalgar. At the Battle of Cape St Vincent (1797) only 73 men were killed.

Compare these statistics with those of the *fatal* casualties in the Royal Navy for just one year, 1810:

Men killed in action	281
Men died of wounds	150
Men lost through wreck, foundering, fire etc.	530
Men lost by accidents	1,630
Men lost by disease	2,592
Total	5,183

Rupture was so common among sailors in the Royal Navy that, over the years 1808–15, an average of 3,714 trusses a year were issued by the Admiralty to support or contain these painful disorders.

A RIVER OF SEWAGE

London has a number of underground rivers including the Fleet, which has served as a sewer for much of the city's history, even when it was an open river flowing into the Thames. By 1290 the Fleet had become so polluted with raw sewage and other foul debris that the monks of Whitefriars complained to the King that the smell of the river was so bad that even their incense could not mask it.

Their complaint had little effect, though. Half a century later the butchers of Newgate were given permission to use the wharf near the Fleet Prison for cleaning entrails. And anyone travelling down the Fleet by boat risked a soaking, though not from fresh rainwater. Houses beside the river had latrines built over the water and, in the words of one chronicler, 'each privie seat is filled with buttock'.

HaZaRDOUS HISTORY

By the middle of the 17th century, and less than 50 years after the Fleet had been cleaned, the river was described as being 'impassable for boats, by reason of the many encroachments thereon made, by the throwing of offal and other garbage by butchers saucemen and others and by reason of the many houses of office [latrines] standing over it'.

CRIES OF THE CONDEMNED

Elizabeth Fry, the Quaker prison reformer visited Newgate Prison for women in 1813. There she found 300 women incarcerated with their children in conditions that were so appalling that thereafter she devoted herself to the improvement of prisons and asylums at home and abroad. On 4 March 1817 she went to see a condemned prisoner and wrote this account of the visit.

> I have just returned from a most melancholy visit to Newgate, where I have been at the request of Elizabeth Fricker, previous to her execution (for robbery) tomorrow morning at eight o'clock. I found her much hurried, distressed, and tormented in mind. Her

hands cold, and covered with something like perspiration preceding death, and in an universal terror. The women who were with her said she had been so outrageous before our going that they thought a man must be sent for to manage her. However, after a serious time with her, her troubled soul became calmed... Besides this poor young woman, there are also six men to be hanged, one of whom has a wife near her confinement, also condemned, and seven young children. Since the awful report came down, he has become quite mad, from horror of mind. A strait waistcoat could not keep him within bounds: he had just bitten the turnkey; I saw the man come out with his hand bleeding, as I passed the cell.

LADIES FIRST

18th-century travellers were not solely at risk from being robbed by men mounted on horseback. From 1735 comes the account of one traveller in Essex.

A Butcher was Robb'd in a very Gallant Manner by a Woman well mounted on a Side Saddle, &c. near *Rumford* in Essex. She presented a Pistol to him, and demanded his Money; he being amaz'd at her Behaviour told her, he did not know what she meant; when a Gentleman coming up, told him he was a Brute to deny the Lady's request, and if he did not gratify her Desire immediately, he wou'd Shoot him thro' the Head; so he gave her his Watch and 6 Guineas.

WOUNDED IN ACTION

Care of the wounded and the treatment of battlefield injuries still bordered on the primitive during the Napoleonic wars in the early years of the 19th century. During Wellington's drive to push French forces out of Spain, Robert Blakeney was badly wounded in the left leg while attacking enemy lines at the river Nivelle. Propped against a tree by a fellow officer, he watched the attack forlornly and then suffered the terrifying ordeal of coming under enemy artillery fire from which he could not escape, surrounded by increasing numbers of dead and dying comrades.

After some hours Assistant-Surgeon Simpson of the regiment appeared. I then got what is termed a field dressing; but unfortunately there were no leg splints; and so arm splints were substituted. Through this makeshift I suffered most severely during my descent. Some of the band coming up, I was put into a blanket and carried down the hill; but as we proceeded down this almost perpendicular descent, the blanket contracted from my weight in the middle, and then owing to the want of the proper leg splints the foot dropped beyond the blanket's edge; it is almost impossible to imagine the torture which I suffered. Having gained the base of the hill towards dark, a cottage was fortunately discovered and into this I was carried...

After the field dressing Simpson departed in search of other wounded persons; and on his report of my wound two or three other medical officers sought me, fortunately in vain, that they might remove the limb. On the fourth day I was conveyed to a place where a hospital was established; but the inflammation of the leg was then so great (it was big as my body) that no amputation could be attempted. A dressing took place which was long and painful, for I had bled so profusely while in the cottage that a cement as hard as iron was formed round the limb, and before my removal it was absolutely necessary to cut me out of the bed on which I lay. After a considerable time passed in seeping with tepid water, the piece of mattress and sheet which I carried away from the cottage were removed; and now began the more painful operation of the setting of the leg. Staff-Surgeon Mathews and Assistant-Surgeon Graham, 31st Regiment, were the operators. Graham seized me by the knee and Mathews by the foot. They proposed that four soldiers should hold me during the operation; to this I objected, saying with a kind of boast that I was always master of my nerves. They now twisted and turned and extended my leg, aiming along it like a spirit level. The torture was dreadful; but though I ground my teeth and the big drops of burning perspiration rapidly chased each other, still I remained firm, and stifled every rising groan. After all was concluded I politely thanked Mathews, carelessly remarking that it was quite a pleasure to get wounded to be so comfortably dressed. This was mock heroism, for at the moment I trembled as I was just taken from the rack.

HaZaRDOUS HISTORY

WHEN HOLY DAYS WERE HOLIDAYS

Working hours were long and arduous in the Middle Ages, but Sundays and Holy Days were days of rest. The Church Courts made sure of this and anyone caught working on a religious day of rest faced a fine.

THE STREETS OF LONDON ARE PAVED WITH...

Walking the streets of medieval London was seldom a pleasant experience. Householders and tradesmen would throw their rubbish and sewage into the street with no thought of what would happen to it afterwards. Many streets had no pavements as we would know them today. The curved surface sloped down on either side to the 'kennels', which amounted to open sewers, and anyone forced away from the higher parts of the street 'went to the wall' and had to tramp through the filth. In 1667, a year after the Great Fire had destroyed much of the old city of London, a master paviour set out a plan to improve the surface of many of the city's uneven thoroughfares. He blamed the dangerous state of these streets on the use of 'unshapely flint stones, which break like glass, or soft rag stone which quickly moulders, or too small pebbles, and all this laid not on sand or fine gravel but on rough gravel soon carried away by the raker [street-sweeper]'. Regrettably for the citizens of London, his proposed improvements were never implemented. The diarist John Evelyn recorded that London streets, even those paved with cobbles, could be lethal when strewn with rubbish and animal droppings, 'So many of the fair sex and their offspring [have] perished by mischance...from the ruggedness of the uneven streets.'

MOB RULE

Before an organised police force came into being in the first half of the 19th century large-scale civil unrest involving tens of thousands of people could erupt in large cities such as London, often resulting in widespread damage and heavy loss of life.

Throughout the first week of June 1780 London was thrown into turmoil day after day by the so-called Gordon Riots. These were whipped up by supporters of Lord George Gordon, MP and leader of the Protestant Association, which was vehemently opposed to the repeal of anti-Roman Catholic legislation. On Friday 2 June Gordon headed a crowd of 50,000 in a march on Parliament where he intended to hand in a petition. However, he lost control and a squadron of dragoons had to be called in. Elements of the mob then broke away to plunder the private chapels of several Roman Catholic ambassadors.

In the coming days more Roman Catholic places of worship were attacked and burned to the ground, but the mob gradually turned its attention from Catholic targets and started a campaign of general destruction. Prisons were attacked and their inmates set free. A distillery was stormed where many rioters became so drunk that they fell into fires that had been started and were burned alive. Downing Street was also attacked, as was the Bank of England, though here the clerks reportedly beat off their assailants using bullets made from melted-down inkwells.

On 7 June 36 fires were blazing in the city at one time. By the following day armed associations of citizens, detachments of horse and foot guards and the militia of several counties had come together and marched on

London to restore order. After a week of mayhem the rioting was quelled and Gordon was arrested on 9 June, accused of high treason. He was acquitted in the end, but 21 ringleaders were found guilty and hanged. The loss of property was estimated to have been £180,000 and some 850 Londoners had died in the riots.

Charles Dickens described the Gordon Riots in his novel *Barnaby Rudge* and the contemporary writer, Samuel Rogers, witnessed the arbitrary way in which the judicial process set about punishing anyone deemed guilty of having taken part:

> I recollect seeing a whole cartload of young girls in dresses of various colours on the way to be executed at Tyburn. They had all been condemned for having been concerned in (perhaps for having been spectators of) the burning of some houses...it was quite horrible.

HaZaRDOUS HISTORY

PIRATES OF THE CARIBBEAN

Piracy was a hazard that threatened seafarers for hundreds of years and even when the Royal Navy began to assert its control of the high seas in the 19th century, merchant ships were still falling victim to attack from pirate vessels. In 1822 Aaron Smith, a young English seaman, was taken prisoner by Cuban pirates when they captured the ship on which he was sailing from Jamaica to England.

The pirates forced Smith to work for them as a navigator and a member of boarding parties. Any display of resistance was answered with the kind of savage brutality for which pirates the world over became notorious. As a warning of what the pirates might do to him, Smith was forced to witness what happened to one of their other victims who fell foul of the pirate captain.

The man was stripped of his clothes, tied up and thrown into the bottom of a ship's boat. Smith was ordered to get in with five of the pirate crew, who were told to row backwards and forwards for three hours up and down a narrow creek that separated the Cuban mainland from an offshore island.

'I will see,' cried he, [the pirate captain] exultingly, 'whether the mosquitoes & the sandflies will not make him confess.' Prior to our leaving the schooner, the thermometer was above ninety degrees in the shade, and the poor wretch was now exposed naked to the full heat of the sun. In this state we took him to the channel, one side of which was bordered by swamps full of mangrove trees, and swarming with venomous insects before mentioned.

We had scarcely been half an hour in this place when the miserable victim was distracted with pain; his body began to swell, and he appeared one complete blister from head to foot. Often in the agony of his torments did he implore them to end his existence and release him from his misery; but the inhuman wretches only imitated his cries, and mocked and laughed at him. In a very short time, from the effects of the solar heat and the stings of the mosquitoes and sandflies, his face had become so swollen that not a feature was distinguishable; his voice began to fail, & his articulation was no longer distinct.

The captive survived only to be exposed to more of the same torment when he refused to disclose details of the mutiny he had been accused of planning. On his own this time, he was left in a boat in the same insect-ridden waters. After a while the pirate captain ordered his crew to open fire on the boat. When their victim was found to be still alive, a lump of iron was tied to his neck and he was thrown over the side to drown.

THE GREAT STINK

Improvements in the sewage system in London, that were completed in the middle of the 19th century, had an unforeseen but deeply unpleasant consequence for anyone who found themselves near the Thames in warm weather. The summer of 1858 became known for the Great Stink that emanated from the river where an unusually hot, dry summer combined with the flow of raw sewage that discharged directly into the increasingly fetid water. The smell became so intolerable that river excursions had to be stopped and the windows of the Houses of Parliament overlooking the river had to be draped with curtains soaked in chloride of lime in an effort to reduce the appalling smell seeping inside. The same problem recurred for a further decade until a more efficient drainage system removed London's sewage down the river and well away from the city.

HaZaRDOUS HISTORY

MAKING THE PUNISHMENT FIT THE CRIME

As late as 1819 people could be hanged in Britain for cutting down a tree in any avenue, garden or plantation; for impersonating a Chelsea pensioner; or for damaging Westminster Bridge. Between 1851 and 1852, 55 boys under 14 years old were sent to prison for stealing less than sixpence.

DOUBLE VISION AND THE GREAT NORTH ROAD

In the late 17th century road travel in England was still slow and uncomfortable. The idea of anyone being in Kent early one morning and in Yorkshire the same afternoon was unthinkable and, as Daniel Defoe recorded in his 1724 travel book *A Tour Through England and Wales*, this seemingly impossible situation saved at least one highwayman from the hangman's noose.

At four o'clock one morning in the summer of 1676 a gentleman was robbed at Gad's Hill in Kent by a highwayman who later became known as

HaZaRDOUS HISTORY

Swift Nicks. With his ill-gotten gains safely tucked away, Nicks set about making good his escape on horseback and headed straight for the Thames estuary which lay a few miles to the north. This he crossed by ferry from Gravesend and once on the Essex shore, spurred his mare into a gallop and raced through Tilbury, Hornden and Billericay to Chelmsford, where he and his horse rested for half an hour.

Back in the saddle, Nicks set off in the direction of Cambridge, forty miles away. From there he continued as far as Huntington, where he and his mare again rested, for an hour this time, and grabbed a bite to eat. A few miles away lay the Great North Road, up which Nicks kept up 'a full larger gallop' until he reached York in the late afternoon.

Successful in the first part of his escape plan, Nicks wasted little time in getting to work on the second. He changed out of his riding clothes and dressed to make himself look like a resident of the city out for an evening stroll. It was essential, for what would become his alibi, that he made himself known to a prominent citizen, so he got into conversation with the Lord Mayor of York, whom he met at a bowling green and with whom he entered into a wager. Towards the end of their chat Nicks made a point of asking his companion what the time was. The mayor took out his watch and told him; it was close to eight o'clock in the evening.

In due course Nicks was brought to trial for the robbery at Gad's Hill. His victim was specific in assuring the court where he had been held up, the date and time of day, and by whom — the accused man in the dock.

The defence, of course, had a different story to tell. Nicks, the court heard, had been over 200 miles away at the time. Several witnesses were called to confirm this, among them the Lord Mayor of York; he well remembered the man who had set a wager with him at the bowling green around eight o'clock in the evening on the day of the robbery.

Presented with such incontrovertible evidence by such an illustrious witness, the jury had little difficulty in acquitting Nicks. After all, it stood to reason in 1676 that no man could be in two places at once and certainly not in Kent at four o'clock in the morning and in Yorkshire a bare sixteen hours later.

HaZaRDOUS HISTORY

DEMANDING SATISFACTION

Despite legal attempts over the centuries to curb duelling, the practice of men fighting each other to settle a matter of honour continued from the Norman conquest into the 19th century.

Duels often resulted from what today might be regarded as petty disputes and, at a time when wounds often became infected and could not be treated successfully, duelling could also be fatal.

A typical example of what could happen was reported from Plymouth in October 1806, when a duel took place between young naval officers. This had been the result of a row in a pub the night before when one officer had tried to extinguish the lights while the other had been dancing with his girl. According to the official account, 'High words arose, and they immediately adjourned to an inn where the challenge was settled.'

The following morning the two officers, accompanied by their seconds, met in parkland near Plymouth. Armed with a pistol each, they aimed at each other and fired. One dropped to the ground mortally wounded by the ball fired by his opponent which had struck the right side of his body, passed through his chest and lodged in his left shoulder.

His body was left at the scene and everyone else hastened back to their respective ships. The dead midshipman's absence was only noticed in mid-afternoon, when a search party was sent to look for him. As the official record blandly stated, 'He was found lying on his back, his hat on, his pockets turned out, and a cane lying across his arm.' He was 18 years old.

WC WANTING

Hygiene in the late 18th century played almost no part in the domestic life of even well-to-do households. The French writer, François de la Rochefoucauld, visiting England in 1784–5 was horrified at the sanitary arrangements in one grand house at which he dined in London.

> Dinner over the wine [when the ladies have retired]: Everyone expresses his political opinion frankly – indecent topics are discussed with excessive freedom. The sideboard is furnished with

chamber-pots and it is usual to relieve oneself, nothing is hidden – I think it is most indecent.

And so it probably was – although this particular visitor conveniently overlooked a startling fact about his own countrymen. When the great French palace of Versailles had been built a hundred years before de la Rochefoucauld's visit to England, there was not a single lavatory in the entire royal residence.

NOW YOU SEE IT, NOW YOU DON'T – SURGERY BEFORE ANAESTHETICS

Before the use of anaesthetics a speedy surgeon was a popular surgeon and few could match Robert Liston for the speed with which he wielded the surgeon's knife and saw. It is said that 'the gleam of his knife was followed so instantaneously by the sounds of sawing as to make the two actions appear almost simultaneous'. He invented the Liston splint for dislocated thighs, which was still in use during the First World War, and wrote a number of books on surgery.

But it is for his operating technique that Liston established his reputation as one of London's foremost surgeons in the first half of the 19th century. It took him just four minutes to remove a scrotal tumour weighing forty-five pounds, whose owner had been obliged to carry it round in a wheelbarrow until Liston relieved him of the unwieldy appendage.

It took Liston two and a half minutes to amputate another man's leg, although his obsession with speed on this occasion also cost the patient his testicles.

Liston did manage a leg amputation in under two and a half minutes, but this operation proved (if none before had) that speed is not everything in successful surgery. In addition to amputating the leg, Liston also hacked off the fingers of the man assisting him and scythed through the coat tails of a respected medical spectator. The results were disappointing. Both the patient and Liston's assistant died of gangrene and the man whose coat had suffered unexpected tailoring is said to have dropped dead from fright. With a little more care and a little less haste the fatalities from this operation would have been cut by two-thirds at the very least.

CHIMNEY DEATHS

Climbing boys were still being used to clean chimneys well into the 19th century, working in conditions that at best were cramped, dirty and dangerous. Children as young as eight were sent scrabbling through dark, soot-encrusted chimneys and in the worst instances died as a result. In 1817 a Committee of the House of Commons heard shocking evidence of what had happened to several climbing boys. This led to the parliamentary recommendation that the use of climbing boys should be prohibited. But the recommendation was not put into effect and children continued to suffer as a result.

HANGED AT THE YARDARM

The death penalty was rarely handed down in the Royal Navy of Nelson's time, largely because of the difficulty of finding enough men to serve aboard His Majesty's ships. When a man was sentenced to death, however, it was for the most serious offences such as mutiny.

Sailors hanged at sea suffered the terrible prospect of slow strangulation as they were hoisted aloft to hang from a yardarm, the outer extremity of a spar from which sails were suspended. If a condemned man was popular with his shipmates they might be able to haul him up fast enough to break his neck. However, some men could not face the idea of being hanged in this way and preferred jumping overboard to hasten their end.

BAD HAIR DAYS

Throughout the 18th century fashions in hair became more and more outlandish. By the 1770s men were wearing long extravagant wigs and well-to-do women were parading hairstyles several feet tall. These were built up on wire frames and pads covered with hairpieces arranged in complex patterns and twists, sometimes decorated with fruit and flowers. Such arrangements were smoothed with pomades made from pig fat to hold them in place, on top of which were dustings of hair powder. Since so much work went into creating these hairstyles, they had to stay in place for several weeks, during which time they were colonised by mites and sometimes mice, which nested in the cosy interior of the elaborate tresses, feeding on the increasingly rancid hair dressings.

HaZaRDoUS HISTORY

Various methods were used to try to keep down the vermin population in hairstyles of this complexity and size. Servants did their best to trap the larger intruders; for smaller ones there were recipes for liniments that could be applied to the hair to drive away pests. One recipe carried the instructions 'Take an ounce of Vinegar, the same quantity of Stavesacre, half an ounce of Sulphur; mix into the consistency of a soft liniment with two ounces of Sallad Oil'.

The mixture produced was highly toxic and the stavesacre referred to is a herb that had been used since Roman times for driving away vermin. It had to be handled with great care; even swallowing a small amount could result in serious poisoning.

WARWICKSHIRE WITCHES

Belief in the sinister power of witches lasted in some rural areas well into the 19th century. Evidence heard at a murder trial in Warwickshire confirmed that a third of the population of the village where the murder had taken place believed in witchcraft. The accused, a farm labourer aged forty, had stabbed his victim, a woman of eighty, with a pitchfork in the firm belief that she was one of fifteen witches he was meant to kill. In his defence the murderer turned to Holy Scripture and quoted verses from the Book of Leviticus:

> A man also or woman that hath a familiar spirit, or that is a wizard, should be put to death; they shall stone them with stones; their blood shall be upon them.

The judge hearing the case took a more enlightened view and told the court that such superstitions would have had no place among savages. The jury found the accused insane at the time of the murder and he was sentenced to be kept in confinement 'during Her Majesty's pleasure'.

GRINDING THE SOUL

Despite the tireless work of Elizabeth Fry and her fellow reformers, the brutal regimes under which many prisons were run were slow to change. Winson Green prison in Birmingham came under the control of hard-line Governor Austin in the middle of the 19th century. The reign of terror and cruelty he pursued was recorded by one member of the prison staff, who resigned in protest and took his complaints, supported by a catalogue of abuse, to the prison authorities. One bitterly cold winter day Governor Austin was seen throwing four pails of water over a prisoner. The man had been sentenced to just 14 days hard labour for begging and was left soaked to the skin for two hours in a dank underground cell.

The chief warder was no better in his treatment of inmates. He was recorded boasting that he had kept some prisoners without food for seven days, strapped into straitjackets and tied to a wall to keep them upright.

Withholding food from prisoners, or placing them on a diet of bread and water, was a standard punishment for anyone who failed to keep up his designated quota at the crank machine, a device fitted with a handle on which a weight was hung. The daily task was usually set at 10,000 revolutions a day: 2,000 before breakfast, 4,000 before the mid-day meal and 4,000 before supper. Juvenile prisoners worked at a crank fitted with a five-pound weight; adult inmates a ten-pound one. To accomplish this, a prisoner was expected to turn the handle through one complete revolution thirty times a minute, or once every two seconds. Few could keep that up hour after hour and those who failed faced the following day at the crank on an empty stomach. In April 1853 one 15-year-old boy, sentenced to three months' hard labour for stealing four pounds of beef, was so brutally starved and punished for failing to keep up his tally of 10,000 turns of the crank that he hanged himself in his cell a little over four weeks after being admitted to the prison.

LADIES OF THE KNIFE

Organised fighting, especially bare-knuckle prize fights, could draw large crowds until such spectacles were banned in the 19th century. For those who took part the rewards could be considerable, though they were often achieved at a heavy price in personal injury. However, it wasn't only men who took part in vicious public fights: the Swiss writer César de Saussure observed an 18th-century fight between two women and sent home an account of their savage combat.

The two women were scantily clothed and armed with two-handed swords, razor-sharp for their last six inches. Beside each of them stood a man with a long staff, ready to separate the women should blood flow. Ringing the combatants was a sizeable crowd of onlookers, including several peers of the realm who led the crowd in placing large bets on the outcome of the contest.

The first part of the fight concluded when one of the fighters, 'a stout Irishwoman' according to de Saussure, received a deep gash across her forehead. While this was stitched and covered with a plaster, the backers of her opponent, 'a small Englishwoman' raised the level of their bets.

The fight began again, this time with each combatant wielding a dagger in her left hand to ward off blows. The Irishwoman was wounded a second time, and while her injuries were attended once again her opponent was rewarded by loud applause and a shower of coins from her supporters.

As the women set to for a third time, the Irishwoman seemed destined to lose. One more deep wound across her neck and throat brought an end to the contest. These were sewn up by the surgeon, but he refused to let her continue. 'A few coins were thrown to her to console her, but the victor made a good day's work out of the combat,' de Saussure concluded.

HaZaRDOUS HISTORY

Prize fighting in the 18th century had a sort of handicap system in which one man took on two women. The same system even allowed for animals to be included in these gruesome contests.

OVERCROWDING

With little money to spare for accommodation many of the poorest people in Victorian Britain lived crammed together in slum conditions where disease and death were commonplace. An official investigation into housing conditions in London in the late 1860s revealed how serious the situation had become.

The investigators examined 1,989 rooms and found them occupied by 5,791 people belonging to 1,576 families. In the worst cases three or four adults of both sexes were found to be lodging in the same room and often sleeping in the same bed.

> I have note of three or four localities, [wrote the author of the report] where 48 men, 73 women, and 59 children are living in 34

rooms. In one room there are two men, three women, and five children, and in another one man, four women, and two children; and when, about a fortnight since, I visited the back room on the ground floor of No. 5, I found it occupied by one man, two women, and two children; and in it was the dead body of a poor girl who had died in childbirth a few days before. The body was stretched out on the bare floor, without shroud or coffin.

A WARNING TO VISITORS

Street crime was as much a problem in the reign of Queen Victoria as it had been in the reign of Queen Elizabeth I, 300 years earlier.

Visitors to Queen Victoria's capital in 1873 would have found this advice printed in *Routledge's Popular Guide to London*, warning of the dangers awaiting the unwary.

In walking through the streets, avoid lingering in crowded thoroughfares, and *keep on the right-hand side of the footway.*

HaZaRDOUS HISTORY

Never enter into conversation with men who wish to show you the way, offer to sell 'smuggled cigars' or invite you to take a glass of ale or play a game at skittles.

If in doubt about the direction of any street or building, inquire at a respectable shop or of the nearest policeman.

Monday is the workman's holiday; Saturday the most aristocratic day for the Opera, Crystal Palace, &c.

Consult the Post Office Directory for addresses of friends who do not live in lodgings.

Do not relieve street-beggars, and avoid bye-ways and poor neighbourhoods after dark.

Carry no more money about you than is necessary for the day's expenses. Look after your watch and chain, and take care of your pockets at the entrance to theatres, exhibitions, churches, and in the omnibuses and the streets.

BLOOD AND SAWDUST – SURGERY BEFORE ANTISEPTICS

Even though anaesthetics were being used for surgical operations by the second half of the 19th century, going under the surgeon's knife was still a grim business.

In contrast to the pristine garments worn in present-day operating theatres, surgeons of Queen Victoria's day habitually wore, according to one contemporary account, 'old frock coats, stiff and stinking with pus and blood', though the more advanced chose to wear a grocer's bib and apron made of non-absorbent material.

When the surgeon and his team were ready the patient was brought in and laid on the operating table. This was covered with a blanket, over which was spread a large brown oilcloth that hung well down over the sides of the blanket. The reasons for this became clear once the operation had started. At the surgeon's feet stood a four-inch high wooden box containing a deep layer of sawdust. Once the operation was under way, this was kicked by the surgeon to catch the greatest torrent of blood as it ran off the oilcloth. When the sawdust became so saturated that it could absorb no more blood, the surgeon would call to an assistant for 'More sawdust', and a fresh boxful was placed under the operating table to replace the box now filled with a bloody porridge.

LABOUR INTENSIVE

The Industrial Revolution may have brought prosperity to factory owners and the nation as a whole, but it came at a terrible price in working conditions for those labouring on the shop floor. In 1832 a parliamentary committee delivered its report into child labour in mills and factories that drew on evidence given by workers such as Elizabeth Bentley, who was interviewed about her life as a worker in a flax mill. For the 12 months prior to her interview she had been working from five in the morning until nine at night, with a 40-minute meal-break at noon. Asked by one of the parliamentary commissioners, 'Your labour is very excessive?' the 23-year-old, who been working at the factory since she was six, answered 'Yes, you have not time for anything.'

Those who showed signs of fatigue faced beatings with a strap. Asked if the strap was ever used 'so as to hurt you excessively?', Elizabeth Bentley replied, 'Yes it is... I have seen the overlooker go to the top of the room, where the little girls hug the can to the backminders; he has taken a strap, and a whistle in his mouth, and sometimes he has got a chain and chained them, and strapped them all down the room.'

The same punishment awaited anyone who arrived late for work. The Bentley family lived two miles from the mill. According to her daughter's evidence, Mrs Bentley was regularly awake at two or three o'clock in the morning to ensure that her children were always on time.

Years of back-breaking work caught up with Elizabeth Bentley when she was 13 and she developed a painful stoop, crooked knees and weak ankles, which in time forced her to exchange working in the mill for eking out a bleak existence in the poor house.

WE PLOUGH THE ROADS IN SPRINGTIME

The 18th century saw a steady improvement in the road network throughout the UK with the construction of well-drained, even-surfaced highways along which coaches and carts could travel at speeds undreamed of in earlier times. However, this degree of modernisation was not universal and pockets of the country still remained cut off by roads that had barely changed in 500 years. As late as 1789 highways in Herefordshire, for example, became impassable to wheeled vehicles of any kind once the rains of autumn arrived. Goods were still transported by packhorse, as they had been for centuries and for six months of the year visits around the country could only be conducted on horseback. As the weather improved towards the end of April every year, Herefordshire roads were levelled once again by top-scraping 'ploughs' drawn by teams of eight or ten horses.